maybe a week
(it's all one poem)

john martone

samuddo / ocean
2012

maybe a week
(it's all one poem)

samuddo / ocean
ISBN 978-1-105-66433-5

maybe a week

(it's all one poem)

for Giselle Maya
& Malcolm Ritchie

driftwood

chick peas

transplanting

truck

axle

duckweed

rain barrels

driftwood

driftwood
all you
imagine

driftwood branch
helps you
up

rain too
coming & going
driftwood

driftwood getting familiar w/ clover

wild
cherry

bush
honey

suckle
drift

wood

maple keys
on maple keys
driftwood

nobody's raft now driftwood

driftwood
fishermen
haven't a clue

all you can show
for today
driftwood

a human climbs
up from the river
all driftwood

there's
only

one
person

there's
only

one
driftwood

dusk — all's either
mother of pearl
or driftwood

one time knew
archaic word
for driftwood

at dusk
human eyes
turn to driftwood

the sun comes to an end in driftwood

the waves' signature driftwood

one thought
& the next
driftwood

chick peas

my hope
south window's
chick peas

all of us
unlikely
chick pea

planting chick peas –
took me
60 years

my bag
of marbles –
chick peas!

not of the cold world chick pea seedling

my day –
one

joint
of a

finger –
chick

pea
seedling

last night's dream
a chick pea seedling's
blanket of roots

chick pea seedlings
you've never seen
the flower

transplanting

first yr finger
then seedling goes in
then close it

squat – calm
clod – of earth
crumbling

transplanting them you lose yr balance

workboots –
of course
pinching

workboots –
of course
they fit

mud-caked
boots – those
anchors

hose springing
a leak in
spring mist

old bones
popping

spring nightfall
shovel still
stands in earth

truck

you have to rent
a truck & haul
it all somewhere

fountain pen & all the rest gone

if you could just
plow the house
under

everything but the driftwood hauled-off

driftwood
& garden
house empty too

emptied out house
& found yr
sweater button

house emptied-out
happens to be
a full moon

axle

dogwood cut-down
prairie's
axle

you dig
out

a tree
stump

and
the day
begins

stump comes out
& burlap
clothes

like anyone else you begin to forget

those hostas don't belong here either

you swing a pickaxe when the churchbells stop

you & a pickaxe all these years

duckweed

this body
isn't yr body
duckweed blooms

the smallest
known islands
duckweed

not even
a fingerprint –
duckweed

duckweed –
time for
bluets

8 minutes later
sunlight turns to
duckweed

forgetting
all people
be duckweed

duckweed bloom
each one
a refuge

surface tension
unbroken
duckweed

duckweed –

stay here

duckweed
getting close
to cosmic rays

duckweed
close yr eyes
& see duckweed

nothing
weighs you down
duckweed

duckweed –
everyone
walks on water

duckweed –
just looking
is drowning

duckweed
a cure
for drowning

walking home
from the river
you walk to the river

nothing to show all those years duckweed

nothing superfluous duckweed

rain barrels

mind all the dirt you've tracked in

this rain barrel another country

an old
roof

rain
barrels

a rain
barrel

at each
corner

just
his size

rain
barrel

how
many
days

of yr
life

gone
into
this

rain
barrel

little
book

rain
barrel

earth's

orbit –
rim of

a rain
barrel

all those
hydrogen bonds
rain barrel

lifting
my

rain
barrel

lifting
my

garden
buddha

rain barrels
& a kayak –
that's his place

all yr sins
no hope but
rain barrels

rain
barrels
prove

there's
no soul

rain
barrels

in
shadows

a rain
barrel
compass

rain barrel
think of all
those toy boats

his riddle –
rain barrel's
also raft

rain
barrels
his

island
home

www.ingramcontent.com/pod-product-compliance
Ingram Content Group UK Ltd.
Pitfield, Milton Keynes, MK11 3LW, UK
UKHW020217250726
13967UKWH00001B/40

9 781105 664335